YOU *meet* YOU

a journal to
UNLOCK, EXPLORE & LOVE
YOUR INNER SELF

avery schein

Castle Point Books
New York

www.stmartins.com
www.castlepointbooks.com

The Castle Point Books trademark is owned by
Castle Point Publishing, LLC.
Castle Point books are published and distributed by
St. Martin's Press.

ISBN 978-1-250-20239-0 (trade paperback)

Edited by Monica Sweeney

Special thanks to Therese Walsh

Images used under license by Shutterstock.com

Our books may be purchased in bulk for promotional, educational, or
business use. Please contact your local bookseller or the Macmillan
Corporate and Premium Sales Department at 1-800-221-7945, extension
5442, or by email at MacmillanSpecialMarkets@macmillan.com.

First Edition: February 2019

10 9 8 7 6 5 4 3 2 1

CONTENTS

It's nice to finally meet
YOU...

THE FIRST IMPRESSION you make on another person can mean a great deal, but making the right impression on yourself should mean a good deal more. *You Meet You* is an opportunity to do away with concern about what others think of you, to take a look inside yourself, and to discover that deep camaraderie, earnest interest, and love for yourself.

In the pages of this book, you'll find opportunities to explore what makes you, you. Through guided prompts, thoughtful meditations, and evocative inspirations, you can drown out the noise around you and find a tranquil space within yourself. Take a thoughtful approach to this journal, one page at a time, and consider the possibility that wisdom and a guiding hand can be found much closer than you think. Find your confidence, your joy, your power—all by taking a deeper look inside yourself.

INSPIRATIONS

knowing yourself

IS THE BEGINNING

of all wisdom.

—ARISTOTLE

SELF-AWARENESS

In the left-hand column below, write down all of the words that describe who you are right now, today. It's okay if you feel stumped; just do your best. You may feel dissatisfied, or as if you've left something undone, but for now, leave the right-hand column empty. We'll circle back to this later, at the end of the book.

music is the language of the spirit.

IT OPENS THE SECRET OF LIFE BRINGING PEACE, ABOLISHING STRIFE.

—KAHLIL GIBRAN

The Right Notes

Consider your favorite song lyrics. Write down some of the key phrases in the song. Now circle the words that speak most strongly to you. What feelings do those words elicit in you? Why do they speak to you so strongly? Do those words reveal anything about your nature?

....

....

....

Now consider a favorite song without words. Close your eyes, and see it. What does the song evoke in you? How does it make you feel? What does it make you long for? What does it bring to mind?

....

....

....

What, if anything, do the songs have in common?

....

....

....

authenticity

MEANS ERASING
THE GAP BETWEEN
**WHAT YOU FIRMLY
BELIEVE INSIDE AND**
WHAT YOU REVEAL TO THE
OUTSIDE WORLD.

—ADAM GRANT

AUTHENTICITY

Do you perceive a gap between the self you project to others and the self you know to be true within yourself? Consider if this is a true gap or rather that you prefer to hold some parts of yourself private while revealing other parts to the public. If there is a distinct gap between who you know yourself to be and the persona you adopt for others, consider the cost of that mask. Is it heavy to hold? What might it feel like to take it off?

Draw the mask below, then go to a mirror and appreciate something about your true face.

OFF THE PAGE

Which story—via a movie, a novel, a play, etc.—would you most like to step into? What draws you to it? Who in the story has your attention? Whose attention would you not wish to have? With which characters do you most relate?

....

....

....

....

If you were writing your own story with these characters, where would you take them? How will you be changed here? How long will you stay?

....

....

....

....

....

....

YOU ARE

the hero

OF YOUR

OWN STORY.

every block of stone
has a statue inside it
AND IT IS THE
TASK OF THE SCULPTOR
TO DISCOVER IT.

—MICHELANGELO

CHANGES

"Blockhead," "heart of stone," and "rocky road" are a few of the phrases that reveal the traditional mindset about stone and its difficult-to-change nature. Change may not come easily for stone, but change is possible with work and the passage of time, as any sculptor will attest. Consider your ability to change. Are you more like stone—slow to change, and only after great effort—or like a more malleable substance like clay?

I am ....

Write down the first memory that comes to mind relating to a significant time of change. Why do you think this memory in particular stays with you?

....

....

....

....

....

....

THERE IS
NOTHING LIKE
STAYING AT HOME
for real comfort.

—JANE AUSTEN

No Place Like Home

What do you love about your home? Is it a feeling, a thing, a room, a view? Is it another person's presence there with you, or memories held within the walls themselves? If possible, sketch something here to represent what makes home *home* for you, be it a small item, a rough scene, or even a color.

IF WE TALK ABOUT
THE GLASS BEING HALF
EMPTY OR HALF FULL,

I WANT TO KNOW
WHAT DOES THE GLASS
LOOK LIKE FROM
*underneath
the table?*

—BRAD THOR

Spun Glass

You have surely asked yourself the age-old question: Is the glass half full or half empty? But let's sink a little deeper into this, and give the question a spin or two. What type of drink does your glass hold? Is it warm or cool? Does a sip of it refresh you? Does the drink change depending on the day, the hour, the moment? Where is the pitcher that will refill your glass? Will you reach for it if you need it, or hold back?

ADMIRATION

Think of a person whom you admire greatly. Who is this person? What role do they play in your world? Hone in on the qualities that make you respect them. How do you wish you were more like them? How are you already like them? Regardless of whether or not they are a public figure or someone you know personally, consider something they have said or done that has inspired you, and write it on the right-hand page.

Now choose one word that encapsulates that quote and write that here:

WE KEEP
moving forward,
OPENING NEW DOORS,
and doing new things,
BECAUSE WE'RE CURIOUS
and curiosity keeps
leading us down
new paths.

—WALT DISNEY

CURIOSITY

What would you like to experience that you have yet to try? What are you curious about? Why haven't you yet taken steps to try it? If you could talk to that thing that holds you back, what would you say? Write that below, then say it aloud three times.

I LIKE CINDERELLA,
I REALLY DO.
SHE HAS A GOOD
WORK ETHIC.
I APPRECIATE A GOOD,
HARD-WORKING GAL.
and she likes shoes.

—AMY ADAMS

THE LIVELONG DAY

How much pleasure do you take in your daily work? How fine a line is there for you between a job completed and a job well done? Do you strive for perfection, or would "perfection" be a waste of time? Do you have a hard time being messy, or is making a mess a necessary part of your work?

Make a mess, just below, with pen, pencil, markers, melted wax, or even a dribble of coffee.

Now draw something beside it—a flower, a piece of fruit, a sketch of a beloved pet—as neatly as you can. Were either of those exercises uncomfortable for you?

smile in the mirror.
DO THAT EVERY MORNING
AND YOU'LL START TO SEE
A BIG DIFFERENCE
IN YOUR LIFE.

—YOKO ONO

Happiness

Jokes, animals, babies, another person's joyful mood—they are often at the root of a smile. Do you find joy in the ordinary? Do you take pleasure in making others laugh, and even work to make that happen? What brings you so much happiness that it can counteract even a dreary day?

SELF LOVE

Is it hard for you to accept compliments? What is the nicest thing anyone has ever said about you? Spend a few minutes listing what you like about yourself—your favorite qualities. How easy or difficult was that for you to do? How many qualities made your list? How does this list about yourself differ from a list of favorite qualities you could create for someone you love? Why do you think that is?

I CAN LIVE FOR
TWO MONTHS
on a good
compliment.

—MARK TWAIN

I ALWAYS WANT
TO STAY FOCUSED ON
who i am,
EVEN AS I'M DISCOVERING
who i am.

—ALICIA KEYS

Discovery

Think of something you wish you could experience over again, for the very first time. How did that experience awaken something within you? Are there alternate ways in which you might recreate that for yourself? Now consider something you've learned about yourself—recently or in the past—that made you glad, and write a paragraph about your memory of that, just below.

raindrops

ON ROSES

&

whiskers

ON KITTENS...

—*THE SOUND OF MUSIC*

My Favorite Things

What is your favorite:

possession _____   time of day _____

hideaway _____   season _____

sense _____   color _____

memory _____   daydream _____

entertainment _____   instrument _____

sound from nature _____   holiday _____

Circle your favorite thing from your list of favorite things. What would you do if it were threatened? Which favorite thing would you be willing to sacrifice in order to save everything else on your list?

_____

_____

What is your favorite aspect of being human? What do you love best about yourself?

_____

_____

_____

STRENGTHS

you gain strength,
courage, and confidence
BY EVERY EXPERIENCE IN
WHICH YOU REALLY STOP
TO LOOK FEAR IN THE FACE.
YOU ARE ABLE TO SAY
TO YOURSELF,
"I LIVED THROUGH
THIS HORROR. I CAN
TAKE THE NEXT THING
THAT COMES ALONG."

—ELEANOR ROOSEVELT

EMERGENCY MUSCLE

Think of an occasion during which you stepped up in a way you never could have anticipated. What did it teach you about your hidden strengths? Have you leaned on that part of yourself since that time? If not, why not?

YOU HAVE TO

participate

relentlessly

IN THE

MANIFESTATIONS

OF YOUR

OWN BLESSINGS.

—ELIZABETH GILBERT

Gifts

On this present, write the characteristics you feel most exemplify who you are. Circle those things you feel others can see, and highlight those things you wish were clearer in your life—for others as well as for yourself.

The Flip Side of Failure

Consider something you tried to attain, but the goal went unmet. Did it make you more determined or leave you reluctant to try again? Did the experience provide you with tools to use the next time, or teach you anything about yourself? If you were able to go back in time and try again, would you take that chance? If your goals have changed, have you considered why that is?

YOU MUST ACCEPT
THAT YOU MIGHT FAIL; THEN,
IF YOU DO YOUR BEST AND STILL
DON'T WIN, AT LEAST YOU CAN BE
SATISFIED THAT YOU'VE TRIED.
IF YOU DON'T ACCEPT
failure as a possibility,
YOU DON'T SET HIGH GOALS,
YOU DON'T BRANCH OUT,
YOU DON'T TRY—
you don't take the risk.

—ROSALYNN CARTER

WE REALIZE THAT
NATURAL APTITUDES ARE
NOT INTERCHANGEABLE,
AND EACH PERSON MUST,
OF BIOLOGICAL OR
SPIRITUAL NECESSITY,
*practice the art
for which he is fitted.*

—GEORGE WILLIAM RUSSELL

Untapped Potential

Think back to your years in school. Were you ever praised for a talent or ability? Did you perform particularly well in a subject? Do you use that particular skill set today? Have you left a potential strength untapped? Can you imagine an intersection between that potential strength and your current existence?

WHEN THERE IS
NO ENEMY WITHIN,

the enemies outside

cannot hurt you.

—AFRICAN PROVERB

PEACE OFFERING

What are you fighting on the inside? Whether it's a personal trait, a memory, or a feeling—extend an olive branch. How can you take care, quell the hurt, or even make peace with that enemy to turn it into a strength?

BEING DEEPLY LOVED
BY SOMEONE
gives you strength,
WHILE LOVING
SOMEONE DEEPLY
gives you courage.

—LAO TZU

A Second Sun

Is there someone in your life who seems always to believe more in you than you do in yourself? Who is that person? How do you feel about their belief in you? Do you rebuff it, or lean into it?

Are you a source of strength for someone in your life? What fuel do you provide for them? How does it feel to offer your gifts, and to see them accepted?

WELL-OILED ASSETS

What is effortless for you that others seem to find challenging?

....

....

Now, think of the things you've worked hard to attain. What characteristics helped you to achieve those goals? Name as many achievements and the characteristics that helped you to attain them as you can, then circle the characteristics that you know have helped you on more than one occasion.

....

....

....

....

....

....

....

....

strength
&
growth

COME ONLY THROUGH
CONTINUOUS EFFORT
AND STRUGGLE.

—NAPOLEON HILL

THE REAL MAN
smiles in trouble,
GATHERS STRENGTH
FROM DISTRESS,
and grows brave
by reflection.

—THOMAS PAINE

LEMONADE

Sometimes we do things we regret, but often we can find a way to make lemonade from the lemons. Spend a few quiet minutes recalling a situation you wish you had handled differently. How might you have said or done something else? How might you have changed the chemistry of the situation, diluted it with more time to think or a more centered response, and then added a sweet note—a cup of kindness or empathy or even forgiveness? How can you remember this recipe, so you might try it the next time you have one too many lemons on your hands?

calm mind

BRINGS INNER STRENGTH
AND SELF-CONFIDENCE,
SO THAT'S
VERY IMPORTANT
FOR GOOD HEALTH.

—DALAI LAMA

Eye of the Storm

Remember a time of chaos during which you remained calm and functional. Did others look to you for leadership? Reflecting back, are you surprised you behaved as you did? What aspect of yourself anchored you to calm? Has that same aspect helped you through other times of trouble?

ALL FOR ONE

Sometimes it takes a village to get something accomplished. Think of a time when you drew strength from and met goals because of those around you. Who helped? How did they supplement your own gifts? How did the experience leave you enlightened or even changed about the strength of the many?

unity is strength...
WHEN THERE IS TEAMWORK AND COLLABORATION, WONDERFUL THINGS CAN BE ACHIEVED.

—MATTIE STEPANEK

be faithful
in small things
BECAUSE IT IS
IN THEM THAT
YOUR STRENGTH LIES.

—MOTHER TERESA

THE SMALL AND MIGHTY

Every task, from the mundane to the complex, relies upon a set of skills. Acknowledge the skills you depend upon that you likely take for granted, from your senses to your reflexes to your instincts. Name the unsung heroes in your toolbox for everyday living, and consider how those heroes work for you in ways you may not think much about. Spend a few minutes in thanks for those gifts.

I BELIEVE THAT
IMAGINATION IS STRONGER
THAN KNOWLEDGE.
that myth is more
potent than history.
THAT DREAMS ARE
MORE POWERFUL THAN FACTS.
that hope always
triumphs over experience.
THAT LAUGHTER IS
THE ONLY CURE FOR GRIEF.
and I believe that love
is stronger than death.

—ROBERT FULGHUM

BELIEFS

What, for you, is stronger than knowledge? What, for you, is the cure for grief? What, for you, is stronger than death?

....

....

....

....

....

What do you value above everything else? How does that provide you with strength, every day?

....

....

....

....

....

....

only I can change my life.

NO ONE CAN DO IT

FOR ME.

—CAROL BURNETT

Empowerment

Think back to an occasion during which you had to step up and become your best advocate, your most faithful friend, to effect real change. Was this an empowering experience for you, or did it make you uncomfortable? Have you been in this position many times throughout your life? Now imagine how your life would be different without your own self-advocacy. Write out a few sentences to describe how it feels when you stand up for your own best interests, and make real change.

WILLPOWER

The ability to pick yourself up time and again, and to persevere in pursuit of a goal, is a true gift. Think about a time when you defied the odds to make something happen. What drove you forward? What fueled your motivation? Is it still there within you, simmering under the surface or even actively pushing you toward new objectives?

failure will
never overtake me
IF MY DETERMINATION
TO SUCCEED IS
STRONG ENOUGH.

—OG MANDINO

know yourself.

DON'T ACCEPT YOUR DOG'S ADMIRATION AS CONCLUSIVE EVIDENCE THAT YOU ARE WONDERFUL.

—ANN LANDERS

An Accounting

Now is not the time for humility. Let's be real about just how strong you are.

Fill in the blanks:

I am awesome at ....

And also ....

And ....

What is your secret weapon—something within yourself? What are you good at that no one knows about? What strengths lie along the road not traveled? What is your kryptonite, and how can you spin it to make it work for you? What do you straight-up love about being you?

RELATIONSHIPS

*your connections to all
the things around you*

LITERALLY DEFINE

WHO YOU ARE.

—AARON D. O'CONNELL

Your People

Name the roles you hold in the most important relationships in your life, whether they be as parent, spouse, friend, grandchild, employee, etc.

Which roles do you feel best about? Which bring you the most satisfaction? Which do you want most to improve? Are there any roles you seek to shed or change drastically? What role do you hope to hold sometime in the future?

Are you someone's "wise person"? Who is yours?

walking with a
friend in the dark
IS BETTER THAN
WALKING ALONE
IN THE LIGHT.

—HELEN KELLER

THICK AND THIN

It is 2 a.m. and the phone rings. Someone needs your help. Who
trusts you to be there for them at such an hour? Who do you trust
if you need someone in a dark hour of your own? When is the last
time you called that person to let them know, in the clear light of
day, in the absence of strife and drama, that you are grateful for
their presence in your life?

even a brief interaction CAN CHANGE THE WAY PEOPLE THINK ABOUT THEMSELVES, THEIR LEADERS, AND THE FUTURE. EACH OF THOSE MANY CONNECTIONS YOU MAKE HAS THE POTENTIAL TO BECOME A HIGH POINT OR A LOW POINT IN SOMEONE'S DAY.

—DOUGLAS CONANT

Short and Sweet

Do you seek connection with people you don't yet know? Do you attempt to engage strangers in pleasant conversation, or prefer to save your social energy for family and friends? When is the last time you had a rewarding interaction with a person you either don't know well or at all?

to live is to choose.
BUT TO CHOOSE WELL,
YOU MUST KNOW WHO YOU ARE
AND WHAT YOU STAND FOR,
WHERE YOU WANT TO GO
AND WHY YOU WANT
TO GET THERE.

—KOFI ANNAN

Chosen Ones

You can spend one year with someone on a deserted island, and can remain connected to one additional person through a telepathic bond. Who will you take? Who will you remain remotely connected with? Why have you chosen as you have?

Uneven Scales

Consider the most uneven relationship in your life—one that draws from your time or emotional energy, but that seems not to give much in return. Alternatively, is there a relationship that is mostly sustained by someone other than you?

What keeps you rooted to these relationships? What do you hold back from them? Can you imagine life without them? How does that imagined absence make you feel?

What do you wish you could say to these people? Why haven't you said that?

NEVER *above* YOU.

NEVER *below* YOU.

ALWAYS *beside* YOU.

—WALTER WINCHELL

YOU DON'T HAVE TO
HAVE ANYTHING IN
COMMON WITH PEOPLE
YOU'VE KNOWN SINCE
YOU WERE FIVE.

*with old friends,
you've got your whole
life in common.*

—LYLE LOVETT

OLD BONDS

Who cared for you while growing up? Who taught you the most?
Who has remained influential in your life?

....

....

....

....

....

What about your longest-held friendship do you love best? What,
if anything, would you change about it? Why do you think it has
stood the test of time?

....

....

....

....

....

....

WHO CARES ABOUT
THE CLOUDS WHEN
WE'RE TOGETHER?

*just sing a song
and bring the
sunny weather.*

—DALE EVANS

CAREFREE

With whom do you share the easiest relationship? Why do you think it seems so effortless? Do you know one another extremely well? Do things never become too serious? How honest are you with one another? What do you love best about yourself when you're with this person? Does anything prevent you from being that way with others in your life?

Sister

IS PROBABLY THE
MOST COMPETITIVE
RELATIONSHIP WITHIN
THE FAMILY, BUT ONCE
THE SISTERS ARE GROWN,
IT BECOMES THE
strongest relationship.

—MARGARET MEAD

SIBLINGS

If you have siblings, how would you describe your relationship with them? Has it changed over the years? What role have you played in creating that change? If you have no siblings, think of a friend who has, at one time or another, felt like a sibling to you. Are you as close today as you once were? How has your relationship changed over time? What is your fondest memory of this person?

WHEN SOMEONE SHOWS
YOU WHO THEY ARE,
believe them
the first time.

—MAYA ANGELOU

Shadows

Who do you avoid because of a past hurt?

Who do you envy?

Does anyone make you feel unsafe?

Has anyone compelled you to keep secrets? What does that cost you?

Have your instincts steered you away from forging a relationship with someone?

Have you ever felt an instant connection with someone, and turned away from it? Why?

HELPERS

Comfort can take many forms, and can even arrive in a casserole dish. How do those around you come together in times of crisis, including those outside your tight circle of primary relationships? How do you respond when you see those outside your circle of primary relationships struggling? Do you watch from afar, or wade in to see if you might find a way to assist?

Have you ever been the recipient of an act of anonymous kindness? Have you paid that kindness forward? How did it make you feel?

WHEN I WAS A BOY
AND I WOULD SEE SCARY
THINGS IN THE NEWS,
MY MOTHER WOULD
SAY TO ME,
"*look for the helpers.*
YOU WILL ALWAYS FIND
PEOPLE WHO ARE HELPING."

—FRED ROGERS

find joy in everything you choose to do.

EVERY JOB, RELATIONSHIP, HOME... IT'S YOUR RESPONSIBILITY TO LOVE IT, OR CHANGE IT.

—CHUCK PALAHNIUK

Seasons of Change

Think about a relationship that would benefit from a change. A change in attitudes. A change in tone. A change in frequency. Any change at all. How great a change would you like to see? What do you think might stand in the way of change? How much energy are you willing to expend to see change done? What will your relationship look like on the other side of change?

in the end,
WE WILL REMEMBER
NOT THE WORDS
OF OUR ENEMIES,
BUT THE SILENCE
OF OUR FRIENDS.

—MARTIN LUTHER KING, JR.

MEMORIALS

Time brings new people into our lives and takes others from us too soon. Who do you miss? What did they bring to your life? How did they make you feel about yourself? What one word would you use to describe them? How did they leave an imprint on your life? How did they help to make you who you are?

Sunny Days

Who is the most positive person in your life? How do you feel when you spend time with them? How comfortable are you in their presence?

....

....

....

....

....

....

....

....

....

....

....

....

THERE ARE
A FEW PEOPLE WHO
genuinely see the best
in everyone.

—KATHERINE PARKINSON

IT TAKES ONE PERSON
to forgive,
IT TAKES TWO PEOPLE
to be reunited.

—LEWIS B. SMEDES

HEALING

Consider a relationship that has sustained an unhealed wound. What concentrates your focus—how you were wronged, how you wronged another, what was left unresolved, or something else?

Do you need to receive or give an apology? Are you the one you need to forgive? Write yourself a letter, and then let it go.

I THINK THE MOST
IMPORTANT THING IN LIFE IS
self-love,
BECAUSE IF YOU DON'T
HAVE SELF-LOVE, AND
RESPECT FOR EVERYTHING
ABOUT YOUR OWN BODY,
YOUR OWN SOUL...
THEN HOW CAN YOU HAVE
AN AUTHENTIC RELATIONSHIP
WITH ANYONE ELSE?

—SHAILENE WOODLEY

Reflections

Do you find it easier to do for others than for yourself? Do you have a hard time accepting help, attention, or praise?

Who knows you best in this world, and what do you think they believe about you? Are you glad to be so well known by them? Do you wish they knew you even better?

Who last heard you say, "I love you"? Who last told you, "I love you"?

Can you genuinely say you love yourself? How easy or difficult is this for you?

Do you hear your own voice? Do you listen?

What tender gesture can you make to yourself today?

DREAMS

your goals
are the road maps
THAT GUIDE YOU
AND SHOW YOU WHAT IS
POSSIBLE FOR YOUR LIFE.

—LES BROWN

Dream Map

Draw a picture of yourself, just below, with a few of your current dreams for yourself. How far are you from each of them? What, if anything, stands between you and them? Time? Skill? Another person? Draw those barriers into the picture, too, then think about what it will take to draw them back out.

I FOUND THAT THE BODY,
MIND AND SPIRIT
are all connected.
THEY ARE NOT
SEPARATE PIECES.

— JUDITH LIGHT

WHOLE DREAMS

What do you dream for your whole self—heart, lungs, limbs,
mind—for today, for a year from now, for ten years from now? Can
you envision the bridge that spans between today's self and your
future self? Do you try to walk that bridge every day?

A Whispered Hope

Do you wake each day with a wild, secret hope? Say it aloud now, or draw what it would mean to you for it to come true, if you can't put it into words.

*every great dream
begins with a dreamer.*
ALWAYS REMEMBER,
YOU HAVE WITHIN YOU
THE STRENGTH,
THE PATIENCE,
AND THE PASSION
TO REACH FOR THE STARS
TO CHANGE THE WORLD.

—HARRIET TUBMAN

nothing is impossible,
THE WORD ITSELF SAYS "I'M POSSIBLE!"

—AUDREY HEPBURN

imPossibility

Consider something you've already accomplished in your life that exceeded your expectations of yourself. Think about the thin membrane between what you believe yourself to be, and what you are capable of becoming. Feel it expand like a lung as you breathe in possibility.

Write down some things you would like to accomplish, that you may not feel at first you can achieve, but that perhaps you can if only you expand your imagination into those ideas.

An Imagined Interview

You have the opportunity to sit with one person from history for an interview. You cannot change history through this interview, but you can learn from this person in a way that illuminates your own life choices. Who will you choose to interview? What will you ask? Write your questions here, then close your eyes and let your mind wander through the many potential answers.

the power of imagination

MAKES US INFINITE.

– JOHN MUIR

*if no one
ever took risks,*

MICHELANGELO
WOULD HAVE
PAINTED THE
SISTINE FLOOR.

—NEIL SIMON

FIT FOR A FRAME

You will soon be visited by a famous painter at your own home. Will you choose a particular room as your backdrop or go outdoors? Will it be a traditional portrait or something abstract? How comfortable are you in this role? What do you hope the painter captures? How do you hope to feel when you look at the final portrait?

VISIONARY

A future self arrives and tells you that many of your dreams have come true, but cannot reveal which have been actualized. What is your most fervent hope?

Examine this future self. How are you different? What have you shed? Where are you, and with whom? What are you doing? What are your new dreams?

learn from yesterday
LIVE FOR TODAY,
hope for tomorrow.
THE IMPORTANT THING
IS NOT TO STOP
QUESTIONING.

—ALBERT EINSTEIN

dreams are the seeds of change.

NOTHING EVER GROWS
WITHOUT A SEED, AND
NOTHING EVER CHANGES
WITHOUT A DREAM.

—DEBBY BOONE

BLOSSOMS

The dreams we have for others can become as important to us as
our own dreams, though our ability to make them come true is
often limited. Imagine the dreams of your loved ones as the wispy
petals of a dandelion. What does each petal represent?

....

....

....

....

....

Blow gently on the petals. Where do you want the wind to take
them? Where do you want them to grow? How important is it for
you to see them blossom?

....

....

....

....

....

Recurring Dreams

Have you ever wished for the same thing more than once, whether on birthday candles, stray eyelashes, shooting stars, or anything else? Which wishes hold most tightly to your imagination? What has prevented them from coming true? If only one recurring wish were allowed to come true, which would it be? Why?

EVERY DAY,
EVERY BIRTHDAY CANDLE
I BLOW OUT,
EVERY PENNY I THROW
OVER MY SHOULDER
IN A WISHING WELL,
EVERY TIME MY DAUGHTER SAYS,
"LET'S MAKE A WISH ON A STAR,"
THERE'S ONE THING I WISH FOR:

wisdom.

—RENE RUSSO

SOME OF US THINK
HOLDING ON
MAKES US STRONG;
*but sometimes
it is letting go.*
—HERMANN HESSE

Making Space

Consider five things in your life you wish you could release.

1. ....

2. ....

3. ....

4. ....

5. ....

Consider five things you'd do with your reclaimed time.

1. ....

2. ....

3. ....

4. ....

5. ....

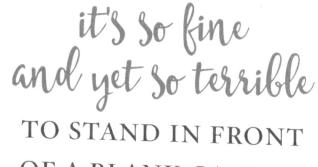

it's so fine
and yet so terrible
TO STAND IN FRONT
OF A BLANK CANVAS.

—PAUL CEZANNE

The Absence of a Guide

Consider the effect of a blank canvas or a pitch-black night. Are you inspired by the absence of stimuli? Does it free your mind? Or does it make you feel anxious, or even afraid? If you could add one thing to this blank canvas, what would it be?

Heavenly Wishes

When you think about life after death, where do your thoughts lead? Do you easily believe, or do you struggle?

....

....

....

....

....

....

If heaven really were a place on Earth, what would it look like? Where would it be? Who would be standing beside you?

....

....

....

....

....

....

....

smiles, tears,
of all my life;
AND, IF GOD CHOOSE,
I SHALL BUT LOVE THEE
BETTER AFTER DEATH.

—ELIZABETH BARRETT BROWNING

THE BIGGEST ADVENTURE
YOU CAN TAKE IS
to live the life
of your dreams.

—OPRAH WINFREY

Big Picture

Thinking back on your inspirations, how might they interact with your dreams?

Focusing on your known strengths, draw a line between them and your most heartfelt wishes for your present-day and future self.

How have your relationships helped or hindered your dreams, including your relationship with yourself?

With a new awareness of your inspirations, strengths, relationships, and dreams, go back to our first exercise (page 5) and fill out the right-hand column, answering this question again:

Who are you, right now, today?

about the author

Avery Schein is a yoga instructor and artist at heart. When she's not working with her students or in her studio, you can find her hiking with her two fur-babies, Joni and Moon. She lives just outside of Seattle, Washington.